The Mushroom Book for Beginners

Second Edition (Revised)

A Mycology Starter

Or

How to Be a Backyard Mushroom Farmer

And

Grow The Best Edible Mushrooms at Home

Frank Randall

@BackyardFarmBks
facebook.com/BackyardFarmBooks
backyardfarmbooks.com

ISBN: 1480086258
ISBN-13: 978-1480086258

DEDICATION

To backyard owners everywhere -
whether a farmer in your heart or just your dreams.

CONTENTS

INTRODUCTION

Are you fed up with paying so much for mushrooms at the store? There is a cheaper way to get them by simply growing your own! Growing mushrooms can be as easy or complicated as you like, depending on the variety you choose, but the end results are most certainly worth the effort involved.

The great thing about growing your own mushrooms is that you can do it right inside your own home or backyard. It's an enjoyable project for families and foodies alike, and all you need to start off is this book, a specialist mushroom growing kit, and a small space in which to grow them!

In this book I aim to teach you the basics about growing mushrooms at home. You'll take a step back in time and learn about the history of mushrooms as food and why it took centuries for home mushroom growing to really catch on. I'll let you know the best types of mushrooms for beginners to grow. If you aren't sure what tools you'll need, don't worry; this book has that covered too. And I'll explain how to make sure that your mushrooms grow quickly and pest free, and share the best ways to harvest, preserve, and store your crop.

I also offer tips on how to set up a mushroom patch in your back yard and answer questions such as whether it's really better to grow them completely in the dark?

So, whether you like shiitakes, Portobello, or oyster mushrooms, stop buying them in stores. I'll teach you how to grow your own and keep your entire family well supplied.

In as little as a few weeks you can grow perfect fresh mushrooms that are ready to eat. Yum!

Best wishes,

Frank

1

THE ANATOMY AND LIFE CYCLE OF A MUSHROOM

If you are going to grow your own mushrooms, you need to be prepared, and that doesn't mean just having the right tools. To truly appreciate and cultivate the best mushrooms, it is important to understand their anatomy and life cycle.

Mushroom Parts

We tend to think of mushrooms as only really having two parts: the stem (or stalk) and the cap (or head). However, there are a few more vital components to mushrooms that you may not notice at first glance.

The Cap

The scientific name for the mushroom cap is the pileus, which helps the mushroom send spores into the air as part of its reproductive cycle.

The Gills

The mushroom gills (lamellae), located on the underside of the cap, have two main purposes. First, they act as a structural reinforcement to support the mushroom cap and prevent it from falling off of the stem. If the cap falls or is broken from the stem, reproduction is likely to fail.

The second purpose of the gills is reproduction. The inner areas of the gills are lined with special reproductive cells called basidia that produce spores. You can think of the gills as being the mushroom's womb.

The Spores

The spores of a mushroom are like the seeds of a flower because they contain the genetic material needed to create new mushrooms. Each mushroom can produce thousands of spores but only a few will actually grow into new mushrooms. This is one of the reasons why it is so important to be vigilant when you are growing your own, which I will cover later in the book.

The Stem

The stem raises the mushroom cap up off of the ground, allowing the spores to be released into the air and blown away, which helps the mushroom population to grow. The potential spore distribution area of mushrooms without stems is much smaller, leading to more competition for nutrients and subsequently poorer growth.

The Mycelial Threads

The roots of the mushroom are called mycelial threads. These small branch-like structures help the mushroom absorb moisture and nutrients from the soil.

The Reproductive Process

The reproductive process of a mushroom varies depending on the type of mushroom, environment, or climate. Many species of mushrooms reproduce sexually, meaning the male and female spores have to find each other in order to start growing a new mushroom. As this type of reproduction can be a little hit or miss, these species will create and eject thousands of spores into the air.

Other species reproduce asexually. Their spores have the ability to basically clone copies of themselves. This does not lead to new mushrooms, just more spores.

Imagine if a woman could clone herself; this would lead to multiple copies of the same woman out there seeking a mate. A mate would still need to be found for reproduction, but the odds of finding one would be improved. The same thing is true for mushroom spores that clone themselves. This process allows them to branch out and find compatible spores. Once two compatible spores find each other they will join and share genetic information, resulting in a mycelium that will eventually become a mushroom.

Life Cycle Summary

The life cycle of a mushroom can be summed up in the following steps:

1. The mushroom drops spores onto the ground.

2. The spores meet compatible spores and germinate.

3. The mycelium forms.

4. A new mushroom grows.

It sounds like a simple process, but it can take anywhere from a few days to a few weeks, depending on the type of mushroom.

Hopefully this chapter has given you an insight into the anatomy and life cycle of a mushroom. With the right tools, the right environment, and the right attitude, you will soon be growing your own delicious mushrooms. All it takes is some time and patience.

Frank Randall

2

THE HISTORY OF EDIBLE MUSHROOMS

Have you wondered how mushrooms made it onto your dinner plate? It's a long story, which starts a few million years ago!

Morels

Morel mushrooms have been around since the dinosaurs roamed the Earth but evidence seems to show that those monster lizards didn't actually like to eat them. It wasn't until early man came along that morels were used as food. Research shows that morels first appeared in the Cretaceous Period and have evolved considerably since then, with 177 different species currently in existence.

Morel mushrooms can be several inches tall, with a cap, or helmet, that is spongy and generally gray or brownish in color. Scientists believe that the distinctive appearance of the morel is what made this species such a popular mushroom to eat. As many mushrooms are poisonous or simply don't taste good at all, the morel was easily identified by appearance.

Morels now grow in many regions and countries, but they aren't usually considered easy to cultivate. Black morels are easiest to find, often in woodlands that have been ravaged by forest fires, leading to people forming morel hunting groups in those areas. Morels are a delicacy and can be worth a lot of money so it's not surprising that people guard their favorite morel hunting grounds closely.

Truffles

Like their cousins the morels, truffles also have a rich history and are considered a delicacy in many different cultures. The ancient Greeks, Romans, and Sumerians were all known for eating truffles and treating them like a treasure! In the royal court of Turin during the 1700s, truffle hunts were often used to honor important guests and dignitaries from other countries.

For reasons that are unclear, truffles became less popular during the Middle Ages but found their culinary place again during the Renaissance, especially in France. King Francis I is widely considered the first French ruler to partake of truffles on a regular basis, but he certainly wasn't the last! Soon all European nobility were enjoying truffles.

In the 19th century, people began trying to cultivate truffles but growing them proved tricky. Truffles tended to grow around oak trees, which led people to grow oak trees in a designated area and hope for the best! Sometimes it worked and sometimes it didn't, as soil, moisture, sun, shade, and other factors weren't easy to control.

Eventually, people learned how to grow truffles, prompting the practice to evolve and expand. The 1855 World's Fair in Paris featured exhibits on truffles and how to grow them. As more people grew them, more people began to eat them. They were still expensive and relatively hard to come by, but they weren't just food for kings and queens anymore.

In the 20th century, the onset of World War I almost wiped out the truffle growing industry entirely. Fortunately, celebrities took up the cause! In 1949 a restaurateur gave Rita Hayworth a truffle and the tradition was reborn. Other fans known to partake in a truffle or two at the time were Joe DiMaggio, Marilyn Monroe, and Winston Churchill.

Thanks to truffle lovers around the world, growth has improved greatly in the last 75 years and truffles remain very popular additions to restaurant menus today. There are now more varieties than ever, including white truffles, black truffles, and even desert truffles, which are sometimes known as Asian truffles. But sadly these delicacies are not easy to grow at home, so this is where we must leave these fabulous little fungi.

Cremini and Portobello

Cremini mushrooms have been popular in Italy since the 1800s, the brown-capped varieties favored over the so-called common mushrooms. The Italians are known for their food, including a multitude of delicious soups and stews, many of which are enhanced by the flavors of the cremini mushroom.

This mushroom became popular in the United States during the 1980s after some marketing magic when fully grown creminis were rebranded as Portobello mushrooms. The cremini mushroom may be a relative latecomer to the menu, but it is now widely grown in the United States as well as countries in Europe and around the world.

Shiitake

Shiitake mushrooms go by a variety of names, including black forest mushrooms, black mushrooms, Chinese black mushrooms, oakwood, and golden oak mushrooms.
Like morels, shiitake mushrooms date back to the days of the dinosaurs and were originally native to what is now Asia. They have been cultivated in China, Korea, and Japan for as long as those areas have been populated but the earliest records of their use in medicine and as food date back to the Ming Dynasty, which lasted from 1368 to 1644 AD.

Not only do shiitake mushrooms taste good, but they are considered by many to have almost mystical anti-aging properties, which is probably another reason that so many people are drawn to these tasty treats.

The Future of Mushrooms

The future of mushrooms as food has never been brighter. Chefs around the world are sharing knowledge and creating more and more mushroom-based culinary delights. Thanks to advancements in cultivation methods and the spread of information and shopping via the Internet, the popularity of all the mushrooms mentioned above is growing in leaps and bounds.

3

THE MUSHROOM GROWING PROCESS

There are thousands of species of mushrooms in the world but only a fraction of that number are good to eat and even fewer are considered particularly tasty or treated as delicacies. Some of the more popular mushrooms include Portobello, morels, and shiitakes but these are also the more expensive varieties.

By growing your own mushrooms you can save money and have an endless supply of tasty treats.

The Mushroom Movement

The Chinese have been growing edible mushrooms for thousands of years. However, the practice didn't spread to other countries until fairly recently because of the fungi's negative reputation and misinformation. In different circles at different times they have been considered:

- Food for nobility
- Food for peasants
- Food of witches
- All toxic or poisonous
- All psychedelic

Of course, none of these beliefs are true and in modern times more and more people are learning how wonderful mushrooms are. There is no place where that is more evident than in the United States.

Mushroom Growing Requirements

Mycology requires only three basic things:

A place to grow

In the mushroom world this is called a growing chamber, even though it doesn't have to be a container with a lid. You can use a bucket, plastic tub, or a plant pot. Some mushrooms actually grow better on logs so you may need to set up the logs or branches in a small area of your yard, in a shed, or even somewhere inside your home. Be aware that the growing environment needs to be a place where you can control the humidity and the temperature. Mushrooms won't grow in the wrong environmental conditions.

Substrate

These are materials that both feed the mushrooms and provide somewhere for the mycelial threads to take root. Some mushrooms will grow well in plain soil but others prefer different substrates, such as rye grain, sawdust, or even damp cardboard!

Spores

You will need a mushroom or spores to begin; a mixture of water and spores in a syringe is a common way to start growing mushrooms in your home.

Most mushroom kits will contain all the essentials to start you off. Check out the ones I recommend on my shopping list at the back of the book.

The Benefits of Growing Mushrooms Indoors

If you live in a region with unpredictable weather, you will have complete cultivating control over the temperature and humidity levels. Indoor grown mushrooms tend to suffer less from pests (more about that later in the book).

Also, growing mushrooms inside from a kit is simple and doesn't need to take up a lot of space. Some mushroom kits only take up a 6" x 6" space, so even if you have a tiny apartment, you can still grow mushrooms like a pro.

Another benefit is that it's fun to watch them pop up and know that you helped! It's a great indoor hobby for anyone stuck inside due to an injury or harsh winter weather. It is also educational and a great family project, as it is easy to get your kids involved in the mushroom growing process. You can help encourage a love of science and nature in them that will last a lifetime.

But my favorite benefit is that you'll have fresh mushrooms close to hand and ready to cook!

Ideal Mushrooms for Home Growth

There are several varieties of mushrooms that you and your family can grow at home. It's best to start with something simple, such as button or oyster mushrooms and maybe morels if you are feeling a little more adventurous. Once you have mastered growing these, you can graduate to slightly complicated projects, such as shiitake, which prefer to grow on logs you can place on your kitchen windowsill or even on your coffee table!

Stay Motivated

The biggest problem with the mushroom growing process is that it takes a lot of time and patience. But if you can stick with it, the rewards will be well worth the effort. Once you get a good mushroom crop going, you'll never want to go back to store-bought mushrooms again.

Frank Randall

4

BEST VARIETIES FOR HOME GROWING

The mushroom varieties most easily grown at home each have distinctive tastes, textures, and differing growing environments. Here's a summary so you can decide which type is best for you.

White Button Mushrooms

In my experience, the best variety for your first crop will be white button mushrooms. They are very easy to grow at home and require minimal amounts of time, effort, and space. Using a white button kit makes it almost impossible to go wrong, as long as you follow the instructions!

Another great reason is their versatility in recipes. They have very little natural taste; however they are great at absorbing the flavors of herbs, spices, and other cooking ingredients. One of my favorite ways to prepare button mushrooms is to simply sauté them in olive oil and butter, freshly ground black pepper, and a teaspoon of a good old fashioned British ingredient, Marmite! (I know it's not that popular here in the United States, but you can get it on Amazon if you are interested in trying it.)

Oyster Mushrooms

Second on the list would be the oyster mushroom. The flavor of this variety can been described as both earthy and sweet. There are several different kinds of oyster mushrooms, each with a distinct flavor so you may want to buy some at the store first to see which variety you like best.

An advantage that makes oyster mushrooms so wonderful to home grow is that they aren't too picky about their substrates. They can grow in several different materials, including sawdust, straw, or coffee grounds.

However, as with any mushroom, you need to keep them in a cool, moist place, such as the basement. They prefer a temperature range between 55 to 65 degrees Fahrenheit, and you can grow them year round. If you don't have a suitable indoor space to grow them, then outdoors is fine. But keep in mind that the mushrooms probably won't appear until fall.

Oyster mushrooms are also nutritionally good for you, filled with vitamins, minerals, and amino acids. So, they can be both a healthy and a tasty addition to your meals.

Shiitake Mushrooms

My third choice would be shiitake mushrooms. However, this variety likes to grow on logs. I suggest you grow from a kit for your first attempt because getting a log that is the correct type, age, and condition for growth can be a little tricky, depending on where you live.

If you are feeling a little more adventurous, I would recommend the following varieties.

Porcini Mushrooms

Prized by chefs and mushroom enthusiasts, this variety carries a higher price tag, but you don't have to worry about that when you are growing your own! They have a unique meaty texture and pungent flavor. Porcini mushrooms aren't as easy to grow inside your home as button or oyster mushrooms, and in my experience are fussier about their cultivation conditions, despite requiring simple sawdust or cardboard substrate and a cool place to grow. They are great fun to watch pop up, and look like fairy tale mushrooms with caps ranging from one to ten inches wide!

Lion's Mane Mushrooms

If you are a seafood fan, you will love Lion's Mane mushrooms, sometimes referred to bearded or tooth mushrooms. They have a very distinctive flavor - a little like crab meat or lobster - and a very unusual appearance. They like to grow on certain types of logs or sterilized sawdust, but are not always easy to grow at home, even from kits.

Portobello / Cremini Mushrooms

Known for their beefy flavor, they are often used in soups, stews, stir fry, and a wide variety of other dishes. If you're looking for a mushroom multi-tasker, the Portobello could be the right mushroom for you - and they are also low in sodium and fat.

Portobello mushrooms grow best in manure-based compost, which you will need to keep replenishing. If you don't have ready access to a supply, you will need to keep buying new kits or spores.

Let Your Knowledge Grow

I would recommend starting off with one of the simpler mushroom varieties to get experience and let your knowledge grow. Once you feel comfortable, don't be afraid to experiment as there are hundreds of different mushrooms out there just waiting to be tried.

Frank Randall

5

SUPPLIES AND EQUIPMENT

If you want to move from growing kits to the more advanced methods of home growing mushrooms, you'll need to familiarize yourself with all of the necessary tools and supplies.

The Growing Chamber

The first thing you will need is a growing chamber, which is the controlled place to cultivate your mushrooms. The exact type of growing chamber you use depends on the type of mushroom you want to grow and also how serious you are about the process.

If you intend to try growing mushrooms as a simple experiment, then just get yourself a plastic bin. If, on the other hand, you want to take the process more seriously, you may need to build or buy a fully automated chamber with temperature and environmental controls.

Substrates

Next, you are going to need the substrates, also called growing mediums. Just as plants need regular soil, mushrooms need particular substrates. The most common include rye grain, sawdust, straw or hay, shredded cardboard and recycled paper. There are also mushrooms that thrive in less traditional substrates such as coffee grounds, bird seed, wood chips, corn cobs, or tree logs.

Spores and Cultures

You need to have mushroom spores or culture to start off - you can't grow them from nothing! The easiest way to get spores is to order them online from a reputable supplier. Check my shopping list at the back of the book for suggestions. Your spores are likely to arrive in the form of a liquid culture, which is a mixture of water and mushroom spores. You can also order live cultures, which may grow faster, but they can be harder to manage properly.

Vermiculite

Depending on what type of mushrooms you are growing, you may want to mix some vermiculite into the substrate. This is a naturally occurring clay-based mineral that can be used as a soil conditioner, helps to encourage growth in certain varieties, and won't contaminate the environment.

Protective Gear

Some mushrooms are very particular and won't grow well in the presence of certain bacteria. This means you may need to wear rubber gloves, or even a full protective suit, if you want growing success.

Sterilization Equipment

This is only necessary if you are not using a kit, but sterilization of the substrates is essential to discourage unwanted mold growth. You'll need canning jars and a pressure cooker to heat the substrates to between 160 and 200 degrees Fahrenheit.

Humidity and Temperature Gauges

Many types of mushrooms need a very specific environment to grow so you need to monitor control the ambient humidity and temperature using a thermometer and a humidity gauge. I've used the Acu Rite Humidity Gauge for a couple of years now and it's a great value, costing around $12.

Petri Dishes

Depending on how precise you want to be, you may need some Petri dishes to grow certain types of mushrooms. The Petri dishes will keep the spores protected until they get big enough to be moved into the proper substrates. If they are unprotected, they are vulnerable to contamination, which could kill them.

Dehydration and Storage Devices

Growing your mushrooms is only half of the battle; the other half is storage until you're ready to cook with them.

As for storage devices, those will vary depending on when you plan to use the mushrooms. If you are going to cook them tomorrow, for instance, a small plastic container would be fine, but make sure that the sides and lid are dark, as mushrooms shouldn't be exposed to too much light.

If you don't plan to use the mushrooms for a few weeks or even months, you have a couple other options. The first and probably easiest is that you can freeze them in appropriate bags or containers, but this does lead to some darkening and marking of light skinned mushrooms, so it's not ideal unless they are to be used in stews or soups.

More information on preserving your mushrooms can be found in **Chapter Eight**.

Frank Randall

6

MUSHROOMS AND LIGHT

Mushrooms won't grow just anywhere, and it's taken hundreds of years for us to develop certain mushroom growing techniques. Luckily for modern day mushroom fans, it is now possible to grow a huge variety of edible mushrooms in your home, but you do need to have the time, the passion, and most importantly, the right location for the mushrooms to grow.

Mushrooms Are Not Plants

Mushrooms are not plants so they don't contain chlorophyll, which means that they don't require a lot of light. You should grow your mushrooms in a fairly shady spot. Too much direct sunlight could heat the mushrooms up too much or even dry them out. Don't allow your culinary dreams to be killed by the sun's harsh rays!

While many species of mushrooms actually prefer to grow in the dark, others can benefit from a little indirect sunlight. Controlled sunlight enables the mushrooms to manufacture Vitamin D, making them more nutritious.

A Side Effect of Light Exposure

If you are planning to grow button or Portobello mushrooms, be aware that the color of the mushrooms will change when they are exposed to the light. This is purely an aesthetic issue and won't affect the taste or quality.

Finding a Dark or Shady Spot

There are two types of home mushroom growing kits: those meant for indoor use and those that are meant for outdoor use.

The perfect outdoor spot is usually in shady. You definitely shouldn't grow mushrooms anywhere that they will get the full brunt of the afternoon sun or get exposed to a lot of chemicals, high winds, or severe weather. Some mushrooms prefer to grow on fallen logs or around oak or elm trees due to the chemical balance of the soil and the shad that these trees can provide.

You can grow shiitake mushrooms and a few other varieties on small chunks of logs inside your home. Whatever the type of mushroom you plan to grow indoors, it should be in a fairly dark place out of direct sunlight. The best option is to grow them in the basement, but if you don't have one, a closet or even a covered bin can do the job, as long as you have the proper air flow.

Choosing a Temperature Controlled Area

The next requirement that mushrooms need is a temperature controlled area in which to grow. If you live in a region where the climate and temperature changes quickly, you might have no choice but to grow your mushrooms indoors.

Most mushrooms like cool places, and as with light control, the best way to control temperature in the house is to grow your mushrooms in a basement, which is generally fairly cool. If you don't have a basement you can create a fully temperature-controlled environment with a homemade incubation chamber and a good temperature gauge. I've used an inexpensive mini greenhouse with great results and there's a link to a similar one at the back of the book.

Controlling the Humidity

The next factor in choosing where to grow your mushrooms is that you need to be able to control the humidity, as mushrooms like moist environments. You might think that the bathroom would be a perfect choice humidity-wise, but that is not the case; there are too many bacteria in a bathroom and far too much light. There is also likely to be unwanted chemicals in the air from bathroom cleaners, hair sprays, perfumes, and other products.

So, once again, the ideal solution is to grow your mushrooms in the basement. If you don't have a basement you can control the humidity in other ways. For example, you can utilize a misting fan or use a spray bottle full of water to keep your mushroom area moist.

Choosing a Safe Spot

As mentioned above, mushrooms can be killed by bacteria, aerosol sprays, and airborne chemicals. They are unlikely to grow in garages or other areas where there may be paint, oil, or other chemical fumes. Mushrooms are very delicate so you should also keep them safe from curious pets or children. Having them plucked, knocked over, or chewed on would definitely ruin your mushroom growing experience!

Frank Randall

7

MUSHROOM PESTS

Growing your own mushrooms at home is a lot of fun but there can be challenges. In addition to requiring the right amount of light, moisture, and the perfect substrates, they must also be protected from pests and molds.

Pests

There are several pests that can attack your mushrooms such as tarsonemid mites that feed on the hyphae of certain varieties. The base of infected mushrooms will turn a reddish color or could break off entirely.

Your mushrooms could also be invaded by tyroglyphid mites. Translucent and small, they like to attack the caps and stems. Easier to spot than tarsonemid mites, these pests invade the visible parts of the mushroom and they leave pits where they feed, which can lead to bacterial contamination of the mushroom causing it to die.

Other visible pests can include eelworms, red pepper, and other mites and flies.

It's worth noting that these pests are more likely to attack mushrooms that are grown outdoors - another good reason to grow them in the house if you can. But do be aware that certain mites make their homes in hay and manure-based substrates, so be sure to thoroughly inspect any substrate you bring into your home from external sources.

Molds

Mushrooms grown outdoors tend to be less susceptible to mold growth, as the ecosystem around them usually helps to reduce mold infestations. Indoor mushrooms can be extremely susceptible to mold problems so it's vital to take proper care of them. Here are some common molds to look out for.

Wet Spot / Sour Rot (Bacillus)

Grain-based substrates in jars can develop a wet spot. This creates a mucus-like slime with a bad odor that smells like burnt bacon, making it fairly easy to recognize. The problem with wet spot is that it is resistant to normal sterilization methods. One solution is to germinate the endospores before sterilizing the substrates. Just soak them in room temperature water for about a day before you sterilize them.

Bacterial Blotch (Pseudomonas tolaasii)

Bacterial blotch is a form of mold that occurs when your mushrooms stay too wet for four hours or more. Bacterial blotch is identified by brown or yellow spots on the mushroom caps.

Shiitake mushrooms are particularly at risk of developing this and similar molds. However, reducing the humidity can control the problem.

Cobweb Mold (hypomyces)

Cobweb mold generally takes hold in wetter mushroom patches, whether indoors or out. This mold's cotton-like webbing can spread through a mushroom jar in just a day or two so you need to be vigilant. Changing the air flow or humidity can help to prevent and control cobweb mold.

Green Mold (Trichoderma harzianum)

Green mold is a big problem for mushroom enthusiasts all over the world, especially in the United States. It can quickly spread over the casing, through the substrates, and onto the mushrooms. Green mold is actually more of a white-colored mass but gets its name from its spores, which will eventually form and spread if you don't remove the infected mushrooms and substrates.

Green mold is not at all easy to treat or control. Your best chance is to prevent it from ever taking hold. If it does appear on your mushrooms, you need to get rid of them, clean and disinfect the entire area, and then start over with freshly ordered mushroom spores.

Prevention

The best way to grow mushrooms at home and not encounter pests and molds is to take the right preventative measures. That means pasteurizing and sterilizing the environment, including the substrates.

Heat is the best way to sterilize most things, including your substrates. For example, let's assume that you want to grow mushrooms in rye grain. All you need is a canning jar, a pot of boiling water, and a pressure cooker.

Put the jar of grain in boiling water for about an hour. Then transfer it to the pressure cooker for another hour or so. The result should be completely sterilized substrates. Just be careful not to heat the substrates too much; extremely high temperatures over 200 degrees Fahrenheit can actually damage your substrates.

Certain substrates, including straw, shouldn't be heated to more than 180 degrees Fahrenheit. It's also worth noting that some substrates should be heated for a longer period of time than others. For example, straw might take an hour or two, while wood chips could take as much as five hours.

You will have to research the proper procedure for whatever substrates you are using and whatever type of mushroom you are growing. If you are going to progress to advanced mushroom growing I would recommend reading 'The Mushroom Cultivator' by Paul Stamets and J. S. Chilton, which can answer any questions you may have after reading this introductory book.

Organic Treatments

Some molds and pests can be treated or prevented with organic treatments. For example, spreading salt can help to prevent green mold while absorbing excess moisture. However, salt may not be a good choice for all mushrooms, so be sure to check beforehand.

Organic sprays can also help reduce risk factors for molds and pests. Garlic spray is an excellent choice because garlic has anti-bacterial and anti-fungal properties and can help to kill unwanted molds. Second, it is natural and completely edible. It may change the flavor of your mushrooms slightly, but garlic goes very well with mushrooms!

Another organic remedy is lavender spray, which controls flies. Simply add a few drops to the water in a mister and spray on your mushrooms.

Starting Over

Unfortunately, prevention doesn't always work all of the time. If you find yourself with a mold or pest problem that won't go away, you will need to remove the infected mushrooms. Sometimes it is better to start over from scratch than to let the problem get out of hand. It can be frustrating, but it may be the best option.

8

GROWING TIMETABLE

Mushroom growing is rewarding, but you do need a little patience. It can take some time for your mushrooms to pop up. Exactly how long depends on a number of conditions.

Inside Versus Outside

Outdoor mushrooms can take months to grow; a year or longer for some varieties. Outdoor mushrooms are also greatly influenced by things like:

- Weather
- Animals
- Pesticides
- Sunlight

The decision to plant mushrooms outside may mean you are in for a long wait, and they may never pop up at all. Outdoor planting for beginners is a bit of a gamble.

With indoor mushrooms, you don't have to worry as much about weather patterns, animal invasions, or pesticides. But as already discussed, you still have to maintain the right environment for your mushrooms.

If you buy an indoor mushroom growing kit, a lot of the hard work will already be done. Those mushrooms should quickly pop up, generally in as little as a few weeks.

Temperature and Humidity

Temperature and humidity have a huge impact on how quickly mushrooms grow. Certain species of mushrooms only thrive within a very specific temperature range. If you control the indoor temperature well you'll see can see fast results. If not, it may take longer for your mushrooms to grow.

Growing Times by Medium

The growing medium also plays a role in how soon mushrooms will grow, and every type of 'bedding' is different. Here are some ballpark time frames.

Logs

Growing mushrooms on logs can take 6 to 18 months, especially if the logs in question are outside. Mushroom patches grown on outdoor logs can come back year after year.

It is possible to grow certain mushrooms, such as shiitakes, on logs in your home. Those can often take far less time to grow, but you are likely to have fewer to cultivate.

Compost

It typically takes about 12 to 15 weeks for mushrooms to grow in compost. However, indoor compost mushrooms may take as little as six weeks. If you want to be eating your freshly grown mushrooms in the shortest amount of time possible, I recommend using an indoor mushroom kit.

Wood Chips and Sawdust

If you sow wood chips or sawdust with mushroom spores, you can see extremely fast results. The less dense growing medium allows the mushrooms to quickly grow and spread, and you can start to see results in as little as three to six weeks.

Growth Times by Species

There are many different varieties of mushrooms and some simply grow faster or slower than others. You'll need to research your particular species.

Oyster Mushrooms

If you buy an oyster mushroom kit, you can expect to wait about one to three weeks to see your mushrooms pop up. There are some oyster mushroom kits that are designed for outdoor growth on logs and others that are designed for indoor growth in straw. Either way, the growth time will remain about the same.

Lion's Mane Mushrooms

Lion's Mane mushrooms will start to grow almost immediately and are fun to watch. Nevertheless, they won't fully mature for about two to three weeks. Many Lion's Mane mushrooms can grow to be about the size of a tennis ball.

Button Mushrooms

Button mushrooms are among the easiest varieties to grow at home, but not the quickest. Be sure to lightly mist your mushrooms with water every two or three days, as this will encourage them to grow. A group of button mushrooms should start to appear within two weeks and be fully mature in about two and a half to three weeks.

Portobello / Cremini Mushrooms

Portobello and cremini mushrooms are very similar to button mushrooms, and they usually take about three weeks to grow.

Shiitake Mushrooms

On average, you should see your shiitakes pop up in about two weeks. Wait to harvest them until they are about three or four inches wide, but never pick them; instead, cut them off at the base. This will leave the entire root system intact so that new shiitakes will grow, giving you future crops.

Morel Mushrooms

All of the action will happen below the surface for the first 10 or 12 days. So, they may appear to seemingly pop up out of nowhere on day 13 or 14.

The Benefits of Mushroom Growing

It may seem like growing your own mushrooms is a lot of work and takes a lot of time - which is true. However, there are a lot of benefits. Just think of the money you will save and how great it will be to have fresh, organic mushrooms right at your fingertips. All of the tasty meals you create with your mushrooms will definitely make up for the time spent.

9

PRESERVING YOUR MUSHROOMS

Growing your own mushrooms can be a great hobby. However, even the smallest of mushroom kits can produce more mushrooms than you reasonably eat before they go bad.

There are many different techniques you can use to preserve your mushrooms, but most fall into three main categories: pickling, drying, and freezing.

Pickling and Salting Methods

Pickling mushrooms is relatively common practice in Europe, particular in Italy. It is less popular in the United States, where drying and freezing are more popular.

The simplest pickling method involves olive oil, vinegar, and a spoonful of salt. Put the salt and a couple pints of vinegar in a pot with some pickling spices. Bring that mixture to the boil and then add the mushrooms to it. Let that boil for several more minutes and then put it into sterilized canning jars immediately. Once the mixture is in the canning jars, cover everything with a good layer of olive oil.

You can use whatever herbs and spices you like. There are some excellent pickled mushroom recipes at **cooks.com**. Just look around until you find one that you think you'll enjoy.

Once you have pickled your mushrooms, you need to periodically check the canning jars for any evidence of mold. The contents of any moldy jars should be quickly thrown away and the jars should be thoroughly cleaned and sterilized before you use them again.

You can dry or wet salt your mushrooms. To dry salt them, pour a layer of course, gritty salt into a glass baking dish. Add a layer of mushrooms and then pour more salt on top. When you're ready to eat them, soak the mushrooms to remove some salt.

Brining, or wet salting, is basically the same as pickling, but uses a lot of salt and some vinegar. Bring the vinegar and salt mixture to a boil and then reduce it to a concentrated mixture that is poured over the mushrooms once they are in the canning jars. Some people think brining leaves the mushrooms rather flavorless, but it depends on the recipe you use. Keep in mind that you can add spices to taste when you are ready to eat them.

Canning food at home is another book altogether, so I've added my favorite title to the shopping list at the back of the book, along with some suitable supplies.

Drying Methods

Dried mushrooms will last a long time because they are pretty much incapable of spoiling. One popular way to dry mushrooms is to string them up using cotton thread - kind of like stringing popcorn to hang on a Christmas tree. Just slice the mushrooms and use a needle to sew them onto the string. Next, hang them up in a warm place to dry. Depending on your particular environment, drying could take as little as eight hours or as long as a couple of days. When they are completely dry, pack them into air tight canning jars.

Another way to dry mushrooms is to cut the mushrooms into slices, then line wire trays with kitchen paper. After about eight hours of drying on trays in a warm place, they should be ready to be packed away in canning jars.

The tray method is excellent if you are planning to dry a large amount of mushrooms. The string method is better if you are only drying a few mushrooms.

Special Drying Considerations

Many of the tastiest mushrooms are still just as good when dehydrated. You may find it helpful to build a simple drying cabinet or a drying shed. Having a designated area just for drying will help lower the risk of contamination and mold. You can slice up the mushrooms and allow them to dry in an oven, or as I recently discovered, treat yourself to an electric food dehydrator. I've used my Nesco dehydrator for six months and now wouldn't be without it.

Freezing Methods

Some varieties of mushrooms freeze well raw. You may want to slice them first, rather than freezing them whole. Other varieties of mushrooms require a little more pre-treatment. You can slice the mushrooms and then fry them with a few herbs and a little olive oil. When you go to freeze them, organize them into portions, that way you can just take out a pack at a time and cook them as needed.

Another way to prepare mushrooms for freezing is to blanch them, which means dropping them into boiling water for a minute or two and then rinsing them in cold water. Prior to blanching, make sure that you get any dirt or debris off of the mushrooms.

Vacuum sealing is also a good way to freeze your mushrooms. When no air is present, the likelihood of spoiling is considerably reduced. The other bonus is that since no air is present, the bags will take up less space in your freezer!

There are many ways to spice and preserve mushrooms. If you are going to grow them, you should definitely be able to eat them when you want, instead of allowing them to spoil.

Frank Randall

10

SHOPPING LIST

You can purchase pretty much everything you need to successfully grow mushrooms at home at Amazon.

To help you out I've gathered together a list of the essentials, in an Amazon Listmania list here…

amzn.to/frankmush

Frank Randall

CONCLUSION

I hope this book has given you insight into growing mushrooms at home and helped you decide if it is a hobby you would enjoy.

As I have done my best to summarize in this little beginner's book, mycology is pretty straightforward if you use a kit, but a little trickier and even more rewarding if you opt for growing the traditional way.

You can't beat the taste of home grown mushrooms with freshly ground black pepper on buttery toast!

Best wishes,

Frank Randall

Ohio
September 2012

ABOUT THE AUTHOR

Frank was born and bred in Bradford, West Yorkshire, England, in 1945. Born into a family of mill workers, he spent much of his free time on the Yorkshire Moors feeding his fascination with wildlife and nature. He later went on to lecture at the BICC. In 1995 he immigrated to the USA and now lives in peace on the shores of Lake Erie, Ohio, with his wife, two dogs, a colony of honeybees, and a menagerie of other critters.

He's the author of Amazon's #1 Best Selling Backyard Farm Books, which include *The Bee Book for Beginners, The Worm Book for Beginners,* and *The Mushroom Book for Beginners* and *The Sustainable Living Book for Beginners.*

@BackyardFarmBks
facebook.com/BackyardFarmBooks
backyardfarmbooks.com

Frank Randall

YOUR FREE GIFT

To get your FREE copy of '**Edible Landscaping**' just visit…

www.backyardfarmbooks.com/GoMush

…and sign up for my free newsletter.

If you have a minute to leave a review of '**The Mushroom Book for Beginners**' at Amazon that would be fantastic!

This URL will take you straight to the review page:

www.backyardfarmbooks.com/mrev

Many thanks.

Frank Randall

Frank Randall

ALSO FROM THIS AUTHOR

Frank Randall

ALSO FROM THIS AUTHOR

The
Sustainable
Living Book
For Beginners

A Self Sufficiency Starter or How To
Be A Self Reliant Homesteader &
Have a Simple Life, Living Off Grid

Frank Randall

Made in the USA
Lexington, KY
23 October 2012